# Just the Way I Am

Krista Horning with Mary Horning
Photographs by Josh Hackney

Just the Way I Am
Text © 2009 by Krista Horning
Photographs © 2008 by Josh Hackney

Published in 2011
by Christian Focus Publications, Geanies House, Fearn, Ross-shire, Scotland, IV20 1TW (www.christianfocus.com)
and
Desiring God Ministries, Post Office Box 2901, Minneapolis, Minnesota 55402 (www.desiringGod.org)
ISBN: 978-1-84550-806-7

Unless otherwise indicated, Scripture quotations are from: The Holy Bible, English Standard Version,
Copyright 2001 by Crossway Bibles, a division of Good News Publishers. Used by permission. All rights reserved.

Other Scripture quotations are from: The Holy Bible, New International Version (NIV)
Copyright 1973, 1984 by International Bible Society, used by permission of Zondervan Publishing House

Revised Standard Version of the Bible, copyright 1952 [2nd edition, 1971] by the Division of Christian Education of the
National Council of the Churches of Christ in the United States of America. Used by permission. All rights reserved.

Design and layout by Schaefer Design Co., www.schaeferdesignco.com

Printed in China

# Table of Contents

To Mom, Dad, Elisa, and Andrew for always being there.
I love you.

*Not to us, O Lord, not to us, but to your name give glory,*
*for the sake of your steadfast love and your faithfulness!*
*Psalm 115:1*

# Before You Begin...

*"Always be prepared to give an answer to everyone who asks you to give the reason for the hope that you have. But do this with gentleness and respect..."*
*1 Peter 3:15*

Every child goes through the "Why?" stage. Kids and questions go together. But it gets tougher when, with doleful eyes, a child asks, "Why don't my legs work like the other kids?!" or "Why did God make me this way?"

Krista Horning is a young woman heaven-bent on helping children find answers. Especially the Answer, Jesus Christ. With a tenderness tempered by her own physical challenges, Krista considers it her life's calling to lovingly lead kids with disabilities beyond their questions to discover just how wise and sovereign God really is. She's done it for years through her own example (you can't spend time with Krista without feeling her courage and quiet joy), and now she's doing it through her charming new book *Just the Way I Am*.

Knowing Krista as I do, I can almost hear her gentle voice on every page, assuring each special-needs child that God genuinely cares... that he's in control... and he had something very special in mind when he created them. And it would be just like my young friend to say, "Jesus is the One who really understands and he's with you every step of the way. Besides, even he asked 'why' when he was on the cross."

Once kids grasp this powerful truth, there's no holding them back—no matter what the disability, their smiles and joy become living proof of their new-found freedom in the Savior. That's Krista's goal behind the book you hold in your hands—she wants every child, she wants all of us to simply trust the One who holds all the answers in his hand. So, please, share *Just the Way I Am* with a little one. Walk a questioning child through its pages. Talk about the photographs. You, too, may end up smiling, not in spite of your physical challenges, but because of them. Just like Krista.

Joni Eareckson Tada
*Joni and Friends International Disability Center*

*Count it all joy, my brothers, when you meet trials of various kinds,*
*for you know that the testing of your faith produces steadfastness.*
*Blessed is the man who remains steadfast under trial,*
*for when he has stood the test he will receive the crown of life,*
*which God has promised to those who love him.*
*James 1:2-3, 12*

# Just the Way I Am

# God made me.

*For you formed my inward parts; you knitted me together in my mother's womb.*
*Psalm 139:13*

# God made me just the way he wanted.

*I praise you, for I am fearfully and wonderfully made.*
*Psalm 139:14a*

# God loves me just the way I am.

*The LORD is faithful to all his promises and loving toward all he has made.*
*Psalm 145:13b (ESV Children's Bible)*

# I have a disability.
# That means God made me different.

*Who has made man's mouth? Who makes him mute, or deaf, or seeing,*
*or blind? Is it not I, the LORD?*
*Exodus 4:11*

I may not walk the same way you do.
I may not talk like you.
I may not even look like you.

*Man looks on the outward appearance, but the LORD looks on the heart.*
*1 Samuel 16:7b*

# But God has a special plan for my life just as he does for yours.

*"For I know the plans I have for you," declares the LORD, "plans to prosper you and not to harm you, plans to give you hope and a future."*
*Jeremiah 29:11*

# He is in control of everything he made, including me.

*Are not two sparrows sold for a penny? And not one of them will fall to the ground apart from your Father. Fear not, therefore; you are of more value than many sparrows.*
*Matthew 10:29, 31*

# Even when I am sad and hurting God is with me.

*God is our refuge and strength, a very present help in trouble.*
*Psalm 46:1*

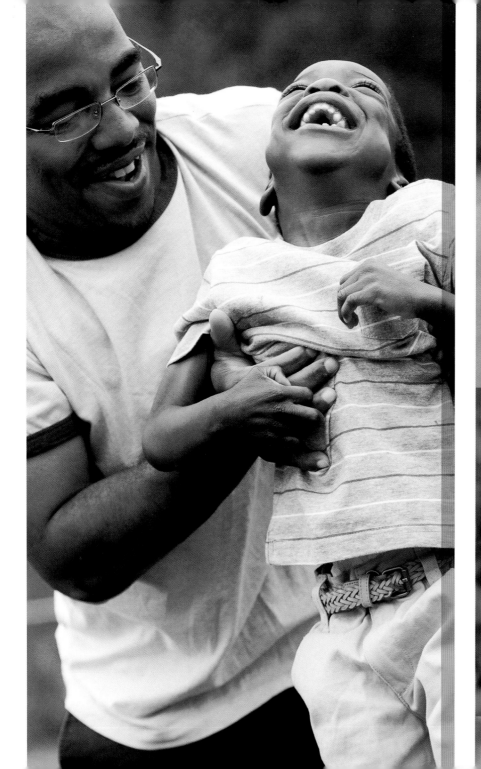

# He watches over me.

*Even though I walk through the valley of the shadow of death, I will fear no evil,*
*for you are with me; your rod and your staff, they comfort me.*
*Psalm 23:4*

# He takes care of all my needs.

*My God will supply all my needs according to his glorious riches in Christ Jesus.*
*Philippians 4:19 (ESV Children's Bible)*

# Most of all, he gave his own Son for my sins.

*But God shows his love for us in that while we were still sinners,*
*Christ died for us.*
*Romans 5:8*

# God made me just the way I am.

*But we have this treasure in jars of clay, to show that the surpassing power belongs to God and not to us.*
*2 Corinthians 4:7*

# There are lots of things I can do.
# There are some things I can't do.

*The parts of the body that seem to be weaker are indispensable.*
*1 Corinthians 12:22*

**God gives me strength to do everything he wants me to do.**

*I can do all things through him who strengthens me.*
*Philippians 4:13*

# I am small and weak,
# but he is great and strong.

*My grace is sufficient for you, for my power is made perfect in weakness.*
*2 Corinthians 12:9a*

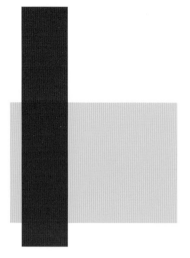

# God made me to glorify him.

*Bring my sons from afar and my daughters from the ends of the earth,*
*everyone who is called by my name, whom I created for my glory,*
*whom I formed and made.*
*Isaiah 43:6b-7*

# He is my greatest joy.

*The LORD has done great things for us, and we are filled with joy.*
*Psalm 126:3*

# I trust him with my whole heart.

*Trust in the LORD forever,*
*for the LORD GOD is an everlasting rock.*
*Isaiah 26:4*

# Someday I will enjoy him forever in heaven.

*You make known to me the path of life; in your presence
there is fullness of joy; at your right hand are pleasures forevermore.
Psalm 16:11*

# God made me with a disability.

*For this slight momentary affliction is preparing for us*
*an eternal weight of glory beyond all comparison.*
*2 Corinthians 4:17 (RSV)*

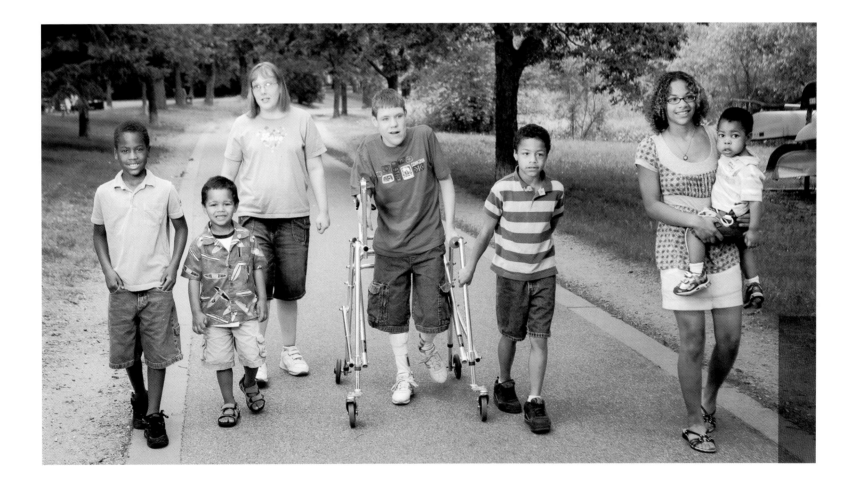

# God loves me just the way I am.

*I have loved you with an everlasting love;*
*therefore I have continued my faithfulness to you.*
*Jeremiah 31:3b*

# From my pastor

*Those who look to him are radiant, and their faces shall never be ashamed.*
*Psalm 34:5*

She had already had more than her share of struggles in the first twelve years of her life, and now she stood on the threshold of those often tumultuous teen years—what would these next years be like for her? She and her family were new at church. I understood her parents had some concerns, so we arranged a time to meet in their home. I had never heard of Apert syndrome before and until that day I had never met a person who had it.

Her face captured my attention but not because of the deformity that I learned was characteristic of this syndrome. I was struck by her countenance and radiance that was reflecting something very beautiful beyond the physical features of her face. The story I heard was not just her story but the story of her parents and all who were touched by this girl's life. The Refiner's fire burned hot and I was getting glimpses of gold.

Perhaps all of this was the result of a defective fibroblast growth factor receptor 2 on chromosome number 10 but the more I heard and the more I observed, the more it seemed that her radiance was reflecting the goodness of a loving Creator who formed every chromosome and intricately knit her together in her mother's womb—a Creator who was lifting up his countenance on her.

The radiance in her face was shaped by words of hope that the Lord had given to the exiles in Babylon through the prophet Jeremiah: "'For I know the plans I have for you,' declares the LORD, 'plans to prosper you and not to harm you, plans to give you hope and a future.'" She had come to know her Creator as the Lord, the God of Israel who has plans for his people. They are good plans with purpose. She embraced Jeremiah 29:11 (NIV) as her own and it was clear that the Lord was using it to give her hope for the future. I could see the hope on her face.

Jeremiah's words in chapter 29 hearken back to his youth when the Lord first spoke to him and said: "Before I formed you in the womb I knew you, and before you were born I consecrated you; I appointed you a prophet to the nations" (Jeremiah 1:5). The Lord plans before he forms and he forms intentionally. He designs, consecrates and appoints with a specific purpose in mind that he established before the foundation of the world. She was not the victim of a chromosomal calamity. She was made with a purpose by an infinitely wise and infinitely good Creator. Children are indeed a gift of the Lord (Psalm 127:3) and this child was no exception.

Nearly a decade has passed since I first met Krista and her family. Her teen years proved to be fruitful and life-shaping. For Krista, Apert syndrome was not a curse to be endured; it was an asset to be invested. Her Maker had a plan for her life and that plan was unfolding before our eyes. Her heart had been uniquely shaped in a way that gave her special understanding, special love, and special influence with other disabled children. She volunteered her time to bless these children and the organizations that serve them.

Our church has many members, and Krista is one of them. There are varieties of gifts and varieties of service. Krista has been given her portion and she has not wasted it. God used her in her teen years for the benefit and building up of his church. Now, among the first fruits of her adult life is this book. It is laden with the truth that brought the comfort and hope still reflected on her face and resident in her heart. May God grant the same comfort and hope to all who read this book and may the fruit of its author's life abound all the more for his glory and the joy of his people to all generations.

*Pastor David Michael*

# Krista's Story

By Mary Horning

Our first child was born in the summer of 1987. I dreamed of being a mother all my life and was thrilled the time had finally come, but I was not prepared for what happened that day. Instead of a newborn's cry as she took her first breath, there was only silence. The doctor held my baby up to me, quickly pointing out her misshapen skull, hands and feet. With concern she could not hide, the doctor told us our child was very sick. "She has obvious defects, which means there may be many more we cannot see." Gasping for breath, our baby girl was hurried to intensive care. Soundless tears fell as the commotion in the room faded and we took in the sobering news.

*Be still, and know that I am God. Psalm 46:10a*

The next day as a surgeon studied her protruding eyes, sunken cheeks, and fused fingers and toes, he concluded she had Apert syndrome, a rare genetic disorder. "This is the worst case I have seen," he told us. "Your daughter has severe bone deformities all over her body which will require years of reconstructive surgery. You may think I can perform miracles and you will walk out of here with a normal child. But that will never happen. The only thing I know for sure is the world will be a cruel place for her." Our hearts ached as the doctor's words went on and on. There would be hearing loss, speech problems, mental delays, and much more. As if all this was not enough, he predicted our marriage would end. Doubt and fear consumed my thoughts. How much pain and anguish can we bear? Why was she born this way? Life seemed hopeless, absolutely hopeless.

*Why are you downcast, O my soul? Why so disturbed within me? Put your hope in God, for I will yet praise him, my Savior and my God. Psalm 42:5 (NIV)*

We chose the name Krista—follower of Christ— before she was born, and now we longed for it to be her identity. But what would the future hold? Would there only be anger toward the God who created her this way, or would she truly follow Christ? I asked the same questions of myself. I had been a believer all my

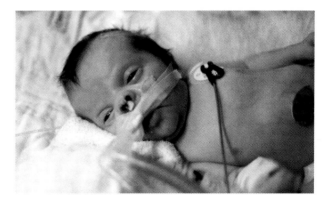

life. Was this how God repaid me for my allegiance? All my hopes for a normal life filled with ballet, piano, and school looked petty now. I was desperate to hear God's voice, just to know he loved me and was still for me. Nothing else really mattered. Clinging to a promise from his word, we dedicated Krista's life to the Lord.

*"For I know the plans I have for you," declares the LORD, "plans to prosper you and not to harm you; plans to give you hope and a future." Jeremiah 29:11 (NIV)*

A nasal bone obstruction made breathing impossible for Krista since infants mainly breathe through their noses, not their mouths. Multiple surgeries to remove the bone and create an airway helped very little, and she remained in the hospital for six weeks until the doctors were confident she could breathe on her own. The day we came home was bittersweet as we set up armloads of medical equipment to monitor her breathing and suction her airway. Now that Krista was home in our care, I lay awake most nights listening to her wheeze and gasp, anxiously begging God for the next breath to come. It was a wintery November afternoon when my fear became reality. Scar tissue blocked one side of her nose. We rushed to the clinic only to be told our surgeon was out of town and no other physicians knew enough about her condition to help. "But what if the other side closes too? She won't be able to breathe."

"There is nothing we can do without your doctor." We wept, walking to the car. If the doctors could not help, who could? As we pleaded with God to show us what to do, our eyes were drawn to graffiti scrawled on the sidewalk: "Trust Jesus."

*I lift up my eyes to the hills—where does my help come from? My help comes from the LORD, the Maker of heaven and earth. Psalm 121:1 (NIV)*

Decision after decision had to be made for Krista's care. Should we subject her to countless surgeries, any of which might claim her life? A team of surgeons performed her most grueling procedure to date when she was four months old. Making an incision in Krista's head from ear to ear, they sawed the skull apart and carefully pieced it back together in a different way to make room for her brain to grow. Family, friends and people we did not even know prayed all day and night. Hours later, when surgery was over, Krista could barely peer through her swollen eyes. Layers of gauze encircled her battered head, hiding gaping holes and bloody stitches. We did not understand this suffering, but all the while God was there with us, quieting our restless souls.

*"When you pass through the waters, I will be with you; and when you pass through the rivers, they will not sweep over you. When you walk through the fire, you will not be burned; the flames will not set you ablaze. For I am the LORD your God, the Holy One of Israel, your Savior." Isaiah 43:2, 3 (NIV)*

Doctor visits were endless; surgery followed surgery. Krista hardly recovered from one operation before going in for the next. At times they appeared to be unproductive, making only slight changes in her quality of life. When Krista was two years old, a specialist examined her fingers, joined together like mittens on her hands. He separated them one surgery at a time, leaving a thumb and three fingers on each hand. Now they were apart, but still stiff and unbending, attached to wrist bones and arm bones and shoulder bones that did not move either.

*So we do not lose heart. Though our outer nature is wasting away, our inner self is being renewed day by day. 2 Corinthians 4:16 (ESV Children's Bible)*

Years later, when Krista was fifteen, we met a doctor who repaired fused elbows by cutting the bone apart and carving a ball and socket joint out of the bone itself. We cringed at the thought of another surgery, another hospital stay, another long recovery. But we knew having the use of one arm would be worth the risk. After surgery, keeping the newly formed joint in motion was critical. She spent three long summer months with her arm in a machine that moved the elbow back and forth, but scar tissue wrapped its way around the joint and made it useless and unmoving like before. Our hearts were broken; all the time and effort, all the pain for nothing. But was it for nothing?

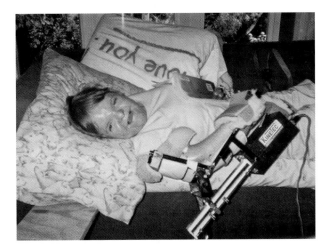

My sinful, rebellious heart often strayed from the truth of God's faithfulness in our lives, but that summer I learned the joy found in God surpassed all the pain we endured. Jesus was enough. He would always be enough.

*For I am convinced that neither death nor life, neither angels nor demons, neither the present nor the future, nor any powers, neither height nor depth, nor anything else in all creation, will be able to separate us from the love of God that is in Christ Jesus our Lord. Romans 8:38, 39 (NIV)*

I was overcome by the weight of God's mercy that was evident in the hard times. There is one day we will never forget. Krista was scheduled for another surgery. Although it was a simple ear procedure, it was at a different hospital than usual, and that added to her fears. On our way there, we sang Bible verses recounting the goodness of God and how he provides everything we need. But I was irritated. Why didn't God just heal her ear? Why did we have to go through this over and over again? As we walked in the door, we discovered that her favorite hospital show, starring Porky Chops the pig, debuted that very afternoon at this new site. Now there was something to look forward to after a painful morning. During the program Krista won a Porky Chops T-shirt, pencil, and key chain. The author and illustrator of her favorite pig book was a guest on the show, and to top it off, a real live pig, the mascot from a local baseball team, walked right into her room for a visit. Krista loves pigs, and that day they showed up everywhere. God did not heal her ear, but he did provide laughter that healed our hearts.

*But this I call to mind, and therefore I have hope: The steadfast love of the LORD never ceases; his mercies never come to an end; they are new every morning; great is your faithfulness. Lamentations 3:21-23*

Krista's facial deformity made her noticeable wherever she went. People stared, pointed, and laughed. "What's wrong with you? Why do you look so funny?" Their taunts stung. Their words hurt. Anger burned inside. I dreaded going to public places since even innocent trips to the grocery store grew into major events. Krista begged to stay home, avoiding the embarrassment and rejection. I shared the heaviness of Krista's hurt and wished I could bear the load myself. Why did people have to look at her that way? Why couldn't they see who she really was? I longed for my girl to have an ordinary face, for the anger to go away. Every day we struggled to listen to God's voice more than the world's. "I know you and made you. You are mine." We held on to his words and gradually saw God had a purpose, even for her disfigured face.

*Indeed, we felt that we had received the sentence of death. But that was to make us rely not on ourselves but on God who raises the dead. 2 Corinthians 1:9*

Living with disability is a daily test: will we find our satisfaction in Jesus? Every day Krista wakes up and still has Apert syndrome. Every day when she looks in the mirror her nose is still crooked and her eyes are still slanted. Every day she relies on our care since her arms do not work and her mental processes are impaired. Every day Krista faces people who dislike her simply because she is different. Every day sin makes us doubt God's purpose and plan. Every day disability affects our lives in a hundred ways. But every day God is good to us. Every day he gives us all that we need. Every day he fills us with grace and mercy and love. Every day we receive forgiveness for our sins through Jesus Christ. Every day God does ten thousand things beyond our understanding that show how great and glorious he is.

*And we know that in all things God works for the good of those who love him, who have been called according to his purpose. Romans 8:28 (NIV)*

In all these years with Apert syndrome, we have known God's greatness in helping Krista endure over sixty surgeries. We have seen his tenderness in family and friends who love and encourage us. We have experienced his grace in preserving our marriage. We have grasped the truth of his Word hidden in our hearts. We have hope and a future. Now I know why Krista was born.

*Though the fig tree should not blossom, nor the fruit be on the vines, the produce of the olive fail and the fields yield no food, the flock be cut off from the fold and there be no herd in the stalls, yet I will rejoice in the LORD; I will take joy in the God of my salvation. God, the Lord, is my strength. Habakkuk 3:17-19a*

# Discussion Questions

1. What is disability? What are some hidden disabilities?
2. What does God think of disability?
3. What can I do to befriend a person with a disability?
4. What talents and gifts do people with disabilities have?
5. Why are people with disabilities important in the church?
6. What can I learn from a person with a disability?
7. How can I serve someone with a disability?

*May the God of endurance and encouragement grant you to live in such harmony with one another, in accord with Christ Jesus, that together you may with one voice glorify the God and Father of our Lord Jesus Christ. Therefore welcome one another as Christ has welcome you , for the glory of God. Romans 15:5-7*

# Quest For Joy: Six Biblical Truths

By John Piper

1. God created us for his glory.

   *"Bring my sons from afar and my daughters from the ends of the earth...
   whom I created for my glory." (Isaiah 43:6-7)*

2. Every human should live for God's glory.

   *"So whether you eat or drink or whatever you do, do it all for the glory
   of God." (1 Corinthians 10:31)*

3. All of us have failed to glorify God as we should.

   *"All have sinned and fall short of the glory of God." (Romans 3:23)*

4. All of us are subject to God's just condemnation.

   *"The wages of sin is death...." (Romans 6:23)*

5. God sent his only son Jesus to provide eternal life and joy.

   *"Here is a trustworthy saying that deserves full acceptance: Christ Jesus came
   into the world to save sinners...." (1 Timothy 1:15)*

6. The benefits purchased by the death of Christ belong to those who
   repent and trust him.

   *"Repent, then, and turn to God, so that your sins may be wiped out." (Acts 3:19)*

   *"Believe in the Lord Jesus and you will be saved." (Acts 16:31)*

# From the Photographer

Two-thirds of the way through my wife's first pregnancy, Krista Horning asked me to capture the photographs for this book. During the course of meeting the families involved in the project, I was struck by the calm and normalcy they exhibited. These families have been through so much, and yet there is joy in their lives. God's grace has allowed these parents to come through difficult times without bitterness. They are able to see past the physical problems and love their children the way God created them. I know that it is hard raising children with disabilities. In the short time I was with them, I could see that their work was sometimes physically demanding and emotionally draining, and yet their care for their children was patient and loving. They didn't have to say a word to exhibit the faith that dominated their lives. What a tremendous testimony they have been given for their Lord and Savior Jesus Christ. I'm thankful to have had the opportunity to work on this book with Krista, her family, and friends, and to have contributed in a small way to helping Krista tell her story.

# Special Thanks

In order of appearance, Giovanna, Cole, Pierce, Darren, McKenna, Paul, Hannah, Micah, Bethany, Nathaniel, Ellisha, Jeremiah, Aaron, Christian, Kempton, Jenifer, Andrew N., Dawson, Andrew H., Joe, Michael, Janet, Naomi, Chris, Hope, Jordan, Brennan, Kaden, Elijah, and Elisa. Your lives tell the story.

David and Sally Michael, for caring about me and this book. I am grateful for your part in my life.

John and Noël Piper, and all in Bethlehem Baptist Church, for loving and living the truth in God's word.

Lukas Naugle, John Knight, Carol Steinbach, and Desiring God, for your dedication, support and the opportunity to publish this book.

Josh Hackney, for your huge commitment to this project and the amazing images you captured.

Anthony Schaefer, for the thoughtful, beautiful way you put it all together.

Joni Eareckson Tada, for your example of joy in Christ through suffering. I am honored you wrote the foreword for this book.

Bethany, Mary, Brenda, and Emily, for your ideas, time, and encouragement.

My family and friends, for loving me just the way I am.

*I give thanks to my God always for you because of the grace of God that was given you in Christ Jesus. 1 Corinthians 1:4*

## ✱ desiringGod

Desiring God exists to spread a passion for the supremacy of God in all things for the joy of all peoples through Jesus Christ. We exist for your joy, because God is most glorified in us when we are most satisfied in him. Please visit our website for hundreds of free and discounted God-centered resources from Pastor John Piper. These resources include books, CDs, DVDs, sermons, articles, and more.

### www.desiringGod.org

On our website you will find hundreds of resources and products to help you find your joy in God. In our resource library you will find sermons, articles, online books, biographies, seminars, and other resources to read, listen, and watch—all without charge. In our store you will find all of John Piper's books and many CD albums, MP3s, and DVDs of his messages available for purchase.

Desiring God
PO Box 2901
Minneapolis MN 55402
Toll Free: 1.888.346.4700
Web: www.desiringGod.org

Joni and Friends is committed to accelerating Christian outreach among families affected by disability in every corner of the globe. Joni and Friends is a bridge of hope and dignity which focuses on meeting the physical, emotional, and spiritual needs of these families in practical ways.

### www.JoniAndFriends.org

Joni and Friends International Disability Center
PO Box 3333
Agoura Hills, CA 91376-3333
1.818.707.5664